P,S. 133Q
248-05 86th Ave.
Bellerose, NY 11426

★ READER'S GUIDE ★

Background

From colonial times to the end of the Civil War, slavery was a fact of life in our nation. In the mid-1800s, times were particularly hard in much of the country. In order to weather these economic struggles, plantation owners often sold their valuable slaves "down South." But being sold to a plantation in the deep South usually meant a much harder life for a slave. Many slaves were driven to desperate attempts to escape.

With no maps to guide them, escaped slaves ran for their lives, heading north to freedom. Abolitionists, former slaves, and other "friends" often helped them along the way. Special signals (such as the words in a spiritual), "safe" houses, and knowledge of their own heritage helped many slaves to create a system of escape. This system became known as the Underground Railroad.

The Underground Railroad helped hundreds of slaves trek their way to new lives as free women and men. Brave souls like William and Callie and those who helped them on their journey paved the way for the freeing of all slaves after the Civil War.

Things to Think About

- How did Callie and William's experiences as slaves differ? Do you think gender made their experiences different?
- Callie and William were determined to escape from slavery. What did freedom mean to them? What does it mean to you? How would your life be different if you were not free?

Things to Do

- The Underground Railroad spanned a large part of the country. Research and map the possible escape routes used and see if slaves may have traveled through your area on their escape to freedom.
- In the book, Callie and William tell their story to their grandchildren. Find out what experiences your grandparents or parents might have gone through that you don't know about. Ask them to tell you about a story from their past.

Places to Go for More Information on the Underground Railroad

FROM THE NATIONAL UNDERGROUND RAILROAD FREEDOM CENTER
http://www.undergroundrailroad.org

FROM THE NATIONAL GEOGRAPHIC SOCIETY
http://www.nationalgeographic.com/railroad/

FROM THE NATIONAL PARK SERVICE
http://www.nps.gov/undergroundrr/

NATIONAL GEOGRAPHIC

Escape to Freedom

THE UNDERGROUND RAILROAD ADVENTURES OF CALLIE AND WILLIAM

BARBARA BROOKS SIMON

PICTURE CREDITS
Cover, 4, 16 (left and right), 17, 22–23, 28, 37 (bottom) The Granger
Collection, NY; pages 1, 6-7, 15, 29, 33 Raymond Bial; pages 2–3, 14
Transylvania Library, Lexington, KY; pages 4–5 ImageBank/Getty
Images; page 6 (left) Courtesy of the Library of Congress; pages 6
(middle and right), 39 Schomburg Center/New York Public Library;
pages 8–9, 30 North Wind Picture Archives; page 9 Chicago Historical
Society; pages 10, 16–17 CORBIS; page 11 (border) Kentucky Museum;
page 11 (bottom) Bettmann/CORBIS; page 12 Morris Library, Southern
Illinois University; pages 18-19 Virginia Historical Society; pages
20–21, 32 Paul Collins/Collins Art; pages 24–25 Jerry Pinkney; pages
26–27, 31 National Park Service; pages 34–35, 37 (top) Ohio Historical
Society; page 36 Archives of Ontario; page 38 Jerry Pinckney/National
Geographic Image Collection; page 40 Nebraska Historical Association.

Library of Congress Cataloging-in-Publication Data

Simon, Barbara Brooks.
Escape to freedom : the Underground Railroad adventures of Callie and
William / by Barbara Brooks Simon.
    p. cm.
Summary: An account of two slaves who escaped from their masters in
Kentucky and, aided by the people of the Underground Railroad, made
their way to freedom in Canada.
  ISBN 0-7922-6551-3
  1. Underground railroad--Juvenile literature. 2. Fugitive
slaves--United States--Juvenile literature. 3. Fugitive
slaves--Kentucky--Juvenile literature. 4.
Slavery--Kentucky--History--19th century--Juvenile literature. [1.
Underground railroad. 2. Fugitive slaves. 3.
Slavery--Kentucky--History--19th century.] I. Title.
  E450.S58 2003
  973.7'115--dc21

                              2003010992

Produced through the worldwide resources of the National Geographic
Society, John M. Fahey, Jr., President and Chief Executive Officer;
Gilbert M. Grosvenor, Chairman of the Board; Nina D. Hoffman,
Executive Vice President and President, Books and Education
Publishing; Ericka Markman, President, Children's Books and Education
Publishing Group; Steve Mico, Vice President Education Publishing
Group, Editorial Director; Marianne Hiland, Editorial Manager; Anita
Schwartz, Project Editor; Tara Peterson, Editorial Assistant; Jim Hiscott,
Design Manager; Linda McKnight, Art Director; Diana Bourdrez, Anne
Whittle, Photo Research; Matt Wascavage, Manager of Publishing
Services; Sean Philpotts, Production Coordinator; Jane Ponton,
Production Artist; Susan Donnelly, Children's Books Project Editor.

PROGRAM DEVELOPMENT
Gare Thompson Associates, Inc.

BOOK DESIGN
Herman Adler Design

CONSULTANTS/REVIEWERS
Dr. Margit E. McGuire, School of Education, Seattle University,
Seattle, Washington
Dr. Russell Adams, Afro-American Studies Dept.,
Howard University, Washington, D.C.

Published by the National Geographic Society
1145 17th Street, N.W.
Washington, D.C. 20036-4688

Printed in the United States of America
13/WOR/3

Table of Contents

Escaping Slavery

From colonial times until the end of the Civil War, slavery was part of life in America. Many places depended on the work of enslaved Africans. But slaves wanted to be free.

Over time, the idea of slavery began to trouble some Americans. Many who were troubled were Quakers, members of the Society of Friends, a religious group. Quakers did not believe in slavery. Some began to help slaves escape. Gradually, an informal network of trails and safe houses grew to help slaves run away to freedom. The network was called the Underground Railroad.

No one is sure how or when the Underground Railroad began. People could not keep records or diaries about it. It was too dangerous to do that.

Railroad terms became a kind of code. Escaping slaves were called *passengers* or *packages*. The people who guided the runaways to freedom were called *conductors*. Hiding places were called *stations* or *depots*.

As more slaves escaped, laws were passed to stop the runaways. Owners posted rewards for escaped slaves. Slave hunters kidnapped runaways for the reward money. The Fugitive Slave Act of 1850 made it a crime to help a slave escape. People who helped slaves escape faced a fine of $1,000 and time in prison. But the lure of freedom was too strong. Runaways continued to follow the Underground Railroad to freedom.

$150 REWA

RANAWAY from the the night of the 2d instan who calls himself *Henry J* years old, 5 feet 6 or 8 in diuary color, rather chunl head, and has it divided side, and keeps it very has been raised in the hous rate dining-room servant. tavern in Louisville for expect he is now in Louis make his escape to a free state, (in all probability to Cinc haps he may try to get employment on a steamboat. He is handy in any capacity as a house servant. Had on w cassinett coatee, and dark striped cassinett pantaloon clothing. I will give $50 reward if taken in Louisvill; one hundred miles from Louisville in this State, and 15 of this State, and delivered to me, or secured in any jail again. WII.

Bardstown, Ky., September 3d, 1838.

RD

scriber, on
negro man,
, about 22
s high, or-
uilt, bushy
stly on one
ely combed;
and is a first
and was in a
months. I
lle trying to
nati, Ohio.) Per-
a good cook, and
en he left, a dark
new—he had other
0 dollars if taken
lars if taken out
hat I can get him
M BURKE

MEET THE PEOPLE

Most tales about the Underground Railroad are **oral histories.** These stories were told *after* the runaways were safe. Callie Taylor and William Ballard escaped from Kentucky using the Underground Railroad. They tell their story after the Civil War. They are now free. Callie's grandmother Martha has joined them on their farm.

Callie, Martha, and William are fictional people, but their stories are like those of many former slaves. This is the story of their escape on the Underground Railroad.

Callie Taylor

Martha Taylor

William Ballard

CHAPTER 1

Callie Runs

The year was 1858. Times were hard in the Bluegrass Country of Kentucky. Many white people lost money. Some had **invested** money in railroads. Now their investments were worthless. Others had bought land. Now no one wanted the land. The price of goods fell. People had no money to spend. Stores went out of business. But one thing still brought a good price—slaves. Many slave owners decided to sell their slaves.

Field hands fetched high prices at **auction.** They sold for up to $2,000. For a **plantation** owner who needed cash, that price was too good to resist. Many of the field hands working in Kentucky were sold farther south. Life on a plantation in the Deep South was harsh. **Overseers,** the men who bossed the slaves, were often cruel. Whippings were common.

Callie lived on the Harrison plantation, Hickory Creek. She had been a house servant, but now that she was 14, she worked in the fields. Callie knew in her heart that she would be sold. Her owner, Master Henry Harrison, needed cash. Rumors spread from plantation to plantation that there would be an auction soon. Callie had to make a decision.

Callie's Story

I knew in my soul that it was time for me to run. Master Harrison kept asking me how strong I was. Well, I was strong. Strong as a bull, but that didn't help me. It meant I'd fetch a high price. And that scared the daylights out of me. Most field hands were sold down South. Once you were sold South, it was the end. My mama and papa were sold South. We never heard from them again. Never. Wasn't gonna let that happen to me. No sir. So, I decided to run. Told Gramma here that was what I was gonna do. No sense her tryin' to talk me out of it.

Gramma heard that folks from a farm about 20 miles away were planning to run. She tried to find out a little more. Soon, one of them folks sent a message to Gramma about where and when I could meet up with them. I was s'posed to head toward the big river and look for a light in the window of a cabin. I didn't tell no one else I was leaving, not even Miss Laura. Me and her had been like sisters. But she was still the master's daughter. I waited till it was dark. I watched the lights in the big house go out one by one. Then I ran.

Slaves knew that the best time to escape was Saturday night. An owner could not advertise for them until Monday. Warm summer nights were a good time to run. Some **fugitives** waited until early fall, when berries and apples would be ripe, and there would be corn in the fields. Now it was late August.

Martha's Story

Callie told me she was running. No sense trying to talk her out of it. Nothing I could do 'cept pray. I told her two slaves down the road ran away, but they got caught. They whipped them something fierce. Their backs were red and raw. Made you sick to look at them. The owners made us watch. They wanted to make sure none of us would run. But that didn't stop Callie.

My heart broke as I watched my little girl run. She wore a dark dress and just disappeared into the night. Tears ran down my face. I knew I might never see my Callie again. If they caught her, they'd whip her and sell her down South. No matter what they did to me, I wouldn't tell. The next day the whole Harrison family was away. Nobody knew Callie was gone till it was too late.

Slaves did not always know how far away freedom was. They had no maps to guide them. They could not read notes to tell them where to go. Still they ran. Many ran away from harsh lives on plantations. Others just wanted to be free.

They traveled by night and stayed off main roads. The forests became their home as they ran north. They had been told that moss grew on the north side of trees. So, they used moss as a guide. Most knew to follow the North Star. Most trusted their instincts. The night became their cloak, protecting them from slave catchers.

Callie's journey to freedom had just begun. She had several miles to go before she reached a safe house. But, unlike many runaways from the Deep South, Callie wasn't too far from the Ohio River and the free states to the north. Each mile brought her closer to freedom.

Callie's Story

That first night, I ran till I thought my lungs would burst. But I didn't dare stop. I went 'cross the fields and into the woods. Branches whipped my face. Finally, I found a cave and crawled into it. I nibbled on a few crumbs of Gramma's cornbread. I tried to sleep on a bed of leaves, but I couldn't. Fear kept me awake.

CHAPTER 2

William's Escape

Many of the runaways were from plantations. Others, however, lived in cities. Some city slaves worked for **merchants,** running errands and delivering goods. Others worked as servants in merchants' homes. Some worked as stone masons or carpenters. Some slaves secretly learned to read and write. Free blacks or Quakers taught them. These slaves heard about the Underground Railroad. They too wanted to be free.

The number of runaways increased in the late 1850s. That caused owners to keep a close watch on their slaves. Many people were in favor of **abolition,** or the end of slavery. As these people fought against slavery, others worked to protect the rights of slave owners. The Fugitive Slave Act of 1850 gave slave owners more power to find and get back escaped slaves. So did several court decisions. Even Northern cities were no longer safe places for the runaways.

Kentucky had more than 700 miles of borders with free states. Large free black and Quaker communities were in nearby Cincinnati and Ripley, Ohio. Freedom, so close, tempted many slaves.

In Uncle Tom's Cabin, *by Harriet Beecher Stowe, most characters were slaves who were cruelly treated. Published in 1852, the novel greatly helped the antislavery cause.*

William Ballard didn't know Callie, but they shared the same ideas about freedom. He worked for a merchant in the central Kentucky city of Elizabethtown. As he ran errands, he noticed signs for an upcoming slave auction. He heard rumors that many "parcels" were being shipped north.

William also noticed that business was bad. Fewer customers came into his master's store. He made fewer trips to pick up goods. Goods stayed on the shelves longer. If his master no longer needed him, William would probably be sold South. William decided it was time for him to escape to freedom.

William's Story

When I saw the sign for a slave auction, I knew it was time to think about an escape. I knew I would fetch a high price. I met with Thomas Smith, a free black man. He was a stone mason. Sometimes my master hired me out to work with him. Thomas hinted that when I was ready to ship out, he would help. But my master watched me like a hawk. I was light-skinned. One time, a customer said he could hardly believe I was a slave. This made my master nervous. But it gave me an idea...

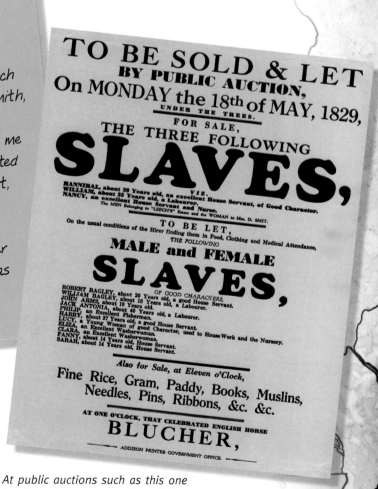

TO BE SOLD & LET
BY PUBLIC AUCTION,
On MONDAY the 18th of MAY, 1829,
UNDER THE TREES.
FOR SALE,
THE THREE FOLLOWING
SLAVES,
VIZ.
HANNIBAL, about 36 Years old, an excellent House Servant, of Good Character.
WILLIAM, about 35 Years old, a Labourer.
NANCY, an excellent House Servant and Nurse.
The MEN Belonging to "LEECH'S" Estate and the WOMAN to Mrs. D. SMIT.
TO BE LET,
On the usual conditions of the Hirer finding them in Food, Clothing and Medical Attendance,
THE FOLLOWING
MALE and FEMALE
SLAVES,
OF GOOD CHARACTERS.
ROBERT BAGLEY, about 20 Years old, a good House Servant.
WILLIAM BAGLEY, about 18 Years old, a Labourer.
JOHN ARMS, about 18 Years old, a Labourer.
JACK ANTONIA, about 40 Years old, a Labourer.
PHILIP, an Excellent Fisherman.
HARRY, about 27 Years old, a good House Servant.
LUCY, a Young Woman of good Character, used to House Work and the Nursery.
ELIZA, an Excellent Washerwoman.
CLARA, an Excellent Washerwoman.
FANNY, about 14 Years old, House Servant.
SARAH, about 14 Years old, House Servant.

Also for Sale, at Eleven o'Clock,
Fine Rice, Gram, Paddy, Books, Muslins,
Needles, Pins, Ribbons, &c. &c.

AT ONE O'CLOCK, THAT CELEBRATED ENGLISH HORSE
BLUCHER,
ADDISON PRINTER GOVERNMENT OFFICE.

At public auctions such as this one in 1829, slaves were sold as if they were pieces of property like the English horse Blucher.

CANADA

LAKE HURON

LAKE ONTARIO

LAKE MICHIGAN

MICHIGAN

NEW YORK

Elgin

Windsor

LAKE ERIE

PENNSYLVANIA

Toledo

Sandusky

Cleveland

OHIO

Ohio River

INDIANA

Westerville

Xenia

Williamsburg

VIRGINIA

Greenfield

Cincinnati

Bethel

Ripley

N

Louisville

Washington

Lexington

Hickory
Creek

Ohio River

Elizabethtown

KENTUCKY

1858

Ohio River

Callie's and
William's route

Free states

Slave states

0   50   100 Miles

0   50   100 Kilometers

TENNESSEE

13

William's Story

My master shipped tobacco to Louisville. Louisville was across the river from the free state of Ohio. First I thought I could hide in the tobacco and ride the wagon as far as Louisville. Then slave catchers appeared in our town. They searched all wagons going out. They found two slaves hidden in a wagon of corn. They were taken away in chains. My heart almost stopped when I heard that. It could have been me.

So, I waited and worked and kept to myself. I did not want to draw any attention. My master locked me up in the store at night. I slept on the floor in the storeroom. The room felt like a cage.

William's Story

One day, my master hired me out to Thomas for some stone work. Thomas said a shipment was going out to Lexington in two days. I would have to make my way from there to the river and Ohio. This might be my only chance to run. I decided to risk it.

The next day, I kept looking over my shoulder as I ran errands. I did not look anyone in the eye. I feared I would give myself away. I could not sleep that night.

The next day, I set out on my errands as usual. I delivered some bills and goods. I did not go back to the store. I met Thomas. He handed me a lady's blue dress and hat. I put them on. Then a white man appeared. He took my arm, and we got in a fancy carriage. I was shaking. The man smiled and said, "Well, daughter, I hope you will enjoy our trip to Lexington." I tried to smile. I was running now. No turning back.

On the way to Lexington, the white man gave William papers saying he had been freed. But William knew it was not safe in Lexington. Someone might know the papers were false. In a farmhouse at the edge of town, another white man, a conductor, gave him clothes that a farmhand would wear. William and the conductor walked many miles to the next spot. William's feet hurt and were covered with blisters.

Runaways used any means to escape. Sometimes they wore disguises. One runaway, Ellen Craft, was very light-skinned. She dressed up like a young white planter, while her husband, William Craft, acted as her faithful servant. Ellen pretended to be ill. She put her arm in a sling to hide the fact that she could not write. The couple somehow had enough money to stay in fine hotels. Finally, they safely made it to Philadelphia. Later, they moved to England. Another slave, Henry Brown, mailed himself north in a box! He shipped himself from Virginia to Philadelphia by express train. His trip took 27 hours!

Ellen Craft

Ellen Craft in disguise

Henry "Box" Brown earned his nickname by shipping himself to Philadelphia in a box to escape slavery.

CHAPTER 3

"Follow the Drinking Gourd"

For slaves escaping to freedom, the beginning of the journey was the most dangerous part. Until they crossed the Ohio River, runaways were in slave territory and on their own.

In Kentucky, only a few white people openly opposed slavery. Runaway slaves had to depend almost entirely on other blacks, free or enslaved. Callie and William were both looking for a freedman named Augustus Garnet. He had bought his freedom and now had a blacksmith shop. Augustus had guided many fugitives to the river and freedom.

Many Underground Railroad routes from the South crossed the Ohio River into the free states of Ohio, Indiana, and Illinois. The river was wide and fast-flowing. Crossing it was dangerous. Many runaways waited until winter, when they could cross on the ice.

Ohio became a major center of the Underground Railroad network. There were several reasons. The state shared a border with two slave states, Kentucky and Virginia. Also, distances north across Ohio to the Great Lakes were shorter than they were in Indiana or Illinois. Many runaways decided to cross the Great Lakes and end their journey in Canada, where they were sure to find freedom.

Harriet Tubman was a famous Underground Railroad conductor. An escaped slave herself, she led more than 300 people to freedom.

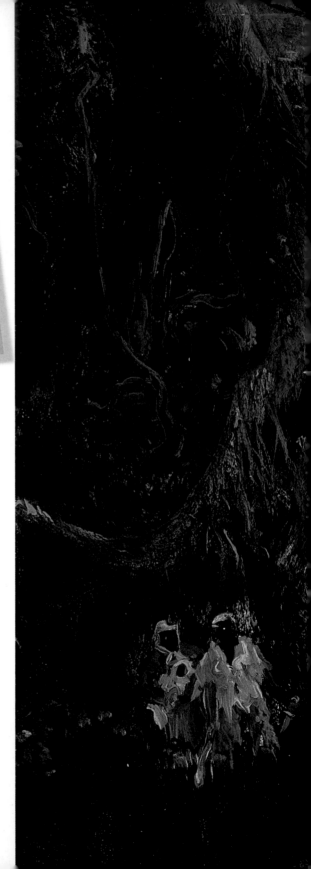

Martha's Story

Once he knew Callie was gone, Master Henry was madder than a wet hen. He carried on something awful. I pressed my lips tight so no words would come out. He didn't beat me. Oh, he wanted to, but his daughter, Miss Laura, bless her, stopped him. He and a slave catcher looked all over the woods. But they couldn't find Callie. She found the underground road! Master Henry sold two of the field hands South. Callie was right to run.

Runaways faced many dangers, from nightly patrols to vicious dogs. Any black person traveling on the road was likely to be stopped and questioned. The countryside itself was dangerous. Swamps and creeks often contained poisonous snakes.

News of a slave's escape spread quickly. White people all along the escape route tried to capture the slave—and get the reward. Still, thousands continued to run away.

John Parker was a former slave who became a conductor on the Underground Railroad. He said that those who ran away were braver and smarter than most. Even if caught and sent back, many tried and tried again. Once they decided to seek freedom, Parker said, nothing would stop them.

Callie's Story

All day I waited in the cave. I knew not to be seen in daylight. Every noise made me jump, for I thought it was someone sent by Master Henry. That night I ran again. I followed the North Star. In my head I sang "Follow the Drinking Gourd," a song about the stars of the Big Dipper. As I got farther on, I felt braver. The night noises didn't scare me. I knew they were just branches in the wind and animals runnin' home. I crossed streams. I used a long stick to chase away snakes. By morning, I figured I was getting near the meeting place. I knew there'd be some kind of a sign.

William's Story

From Lexington, it would have been quicker to follow the road. But even with fake papers, it was too dangerous. My guide took me as far as a patch of blackberries. He drew a rough map of the way to the meeting place. How I wished for a lantern to light my way! The woods were the darkest place I'd ever been. The night seemed endless. Dawn was breaking when I saw cabins in a clearing. Which one was the safe house? I saw some white stones in a circle in front of one of them. I figured that must be a sign. I chose that one.

Callie's Story

I made it to the clearing and the safe house. I heard a low voice calling me, and I headed for the corncrib behind the cabin. When I slipped inside, I met the guide, Augustus. I also met Seth, Rachel, and her little boy. They were runaways too. We were nervous at first. We had no idea what we'd go through together. Seth was a big fellow, a lot like other field hands I'd known.

Rachel was only 30 years old then, but she looked like an old woman. There were awful scars on her legs and back. Her owners had treated her bad.

Then William came. He was different. You could tell he was from the city. He was all shaky from coming through the woods. Twigs and leaves stuck to his hair. He didn't even notice them.

Augustus whispered that we'd wait till dark, then head for the river. We stayed in the corncrib. Rachel's little boy cried. When William told him a story, he stopped crying. I could hardly wait. I wanted freedom so much I could almost taste it!

William's Story

It finally got dark enough to set out. The woods scared me more than the slave catchers. I jumped a foot when something screamed right over my head. Callie laughed and said it was just an owl. I was used to train whistles at night, not large birds! I imagined bears and snakes and all kinds of critters. The others seemed at home in the woods. I just kept telling myself we were on our way to freedom. I'd spent weeks planning this escape. I was not going to let the woods stop me.

When Callie was guided by a song, she was following her African **heritage.** Many slaves, or their **ancestors,** had come from West Africa. Music had played a large part in the **traditions** of West Africa. It became an important part of slave culture too. Songs took on new meanings. White owners and overseers did not pay attention to the songs their slaves sang. They thought music helped slaves work harder. African Americans could send messages through songs. Few white people noticed.

Music provided entertainment as well as a way to send messages.

CHAPTER 4

Steal Away, Steal Away

Some escaping slaves knew the hidden meanings in songs. One important song was "Follow the Drinking Gourd." As Callie knew when she ran, the "drinking gourd" was the Big Dipper. Its "pointer stars" point to the North Star in the Little Dipper. Religious songs, or **spirituals,** often carried information. One song with a double meaning was "Steal Away to Jesus." To *steal away* means "to move secretly." *Jesus* stood for freedom in the North. Another spiritual turned out to be a lifesaver for Callie.

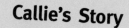

Callie's Story

Have you ever heard of someone being saved by a song? Well, we were. We had just stopped at the edge of the woods. Folks were picking corn in the fields. All of a sudden, they started in singing: "Wade in the water, children. God's gonna trouble the water." We knew that message was for us. It meant that the patrols and their dogs were near!

Augustus knew just what to do. He quick climbed down the bank into a little crick, and we followed him. As long as we were in the water, the dogs couldn't catch our smell and follow us. I think William was more a-scared of the swampy water than of the dogs. We hid for a time under an old covered bridge, then went on toward the river.

Directly across the river was Ripley, Ohio, the goal of many freedom seekers. It was a busy and prosperous river port, with a mill and boatyard. An active group of **abolitionists** lived in Ripley. But many others in town supported slavery. Suspicious neighbors often demanded to search a house for fugitives. Slave catchers were constantly on watch. In spite of this, hundreds of slaves escaped by this route.

William's Story

I surely do hate swamps, as snakes live in 'em! But what scared me most was those horrible dogs barking. I thought we were goners, and would never reach the river. I could imagine the pain of a whip on my back. And even though I was getting more used to the woods, I still jumped every time an owl hooted. Callie liked the woods then and still does. I was just waiting and hoping to get to a town where I'd feel at home. Seth was fine, just like Callie. He was used to a rough life. That life had made him strong too. He carried Rachel and her son across the creek and didn't even breathe hard.

We were lucky that Augustus was such an old hand as a conductor. Since the patrols were around, he took another route to the river. It felt dangerous, but I trusted him. Late that night, we passed quietly through the town of Washington, where the slave market was. Seeing the auction block upset Callie. She'd had a narrow escape.

John Parker was one hero of the Underground Railroad who lived in Ripley. Once enslaved, Parker had bought his freedom for $2,000. From 1845 to 1865, he rescued escaping slaves. Many nights, he made trips across the river to Kentucky in his small boat. Parker sent fugitives to friendly houses in town. Most famous was Liberty Hill, home of the Reverend John Rankin. Rankin was so famous as an abolitionist that angry slave owners offered a reward for his kidnapping.

William's Story

Finally, we were at the Ohio River. Augustus said John Parker was to be there at midnight. He would take us across and to a safe house in Ripley. Augustus whispered directions to Callie and me. Then he disappeared into the woods. Rachel moaned, afraid we had been left. It took us a long time to quiet her.

Callie's Story

We waited and waited in the dark for hours and hours. Finally, there was John Parker. "Five of you? That's right." He pointed across the river. "You see that beacon light on the hill across the river?" he said. "That's the Rankin house. Folks call it Liberty Hill. You ladies will be staying there. Don't worry. Rankin's sons are good with rifles and will keep the slave catchers away. In a few days, we'll see you on your way."

He rowed Rachel, her boy, and me across the river in his skiff. The currents wanted to pull us downstream, but Mr. Parker knew how to handle his boat. We climbed up the back way to Liberty Hill. Then he went back for Seth and William. I'll never forget that beautiful August morning in 1858! We were in the free state of Ohio!

Reverend John Rankin and his wife

William's Story

When Parker rowed away with the others, Seth and I wondered if he would really come back. But he soon returned and brought us across the river to the house of Tom McCague. Mr. McCague was a pork merchant. His cook gave us a fine meal of smoked ham, greens, and cider. What a treat after days of eating dry cornbread! And I slept on a cotton mattress, not on leaves. Best of all, there were no woods noises to keep me awake.

Next day, Reverend Rankin's sons sent over suits of clothing. Seth and I began to look and feel like free men.

Martha's Story

We was at prayer meetin' when the preacher whispered something to me about a package arriving safely. I burst into tears, but couldn't tell anybody why. When I knew my Callie was safe across the river in a free state, I felt almost free myself! Every night I fell on my knees and thanked the good Lord!

The Rankin House on Liberty Hill

27

Even across the river, they were not yet safe. Patrols and slave hunters were active everywhere north and south of the river. Many people in southern Ohio sympathized with slave owners across the river in Kentucky. Callie, William, and the others would travel many more miles and many more days before they could feel truly safe.

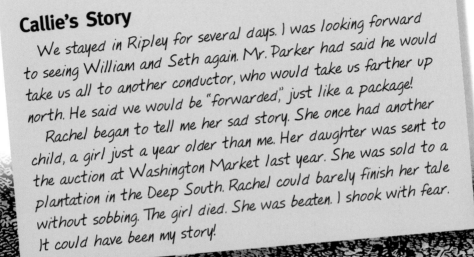

Callie's Story

We stayed in Ripley for several days. I was looking forward to seeing William and Seth again. Mr. Parker had said he would take us all to another conductor, who would take us farther up north. He said we would be "forwarded," just like a package! Rachel began to tell me her sad story. She once had another child, a girl just a year older than me. Her daughter was sent to the auction at Washington Market last year. She was sold to a plantation in the Deep South. Rachel could barely finish her tale without sobbing. The girl died. She was beaten. I shook with fear. It could have been my story!

CHAPTER 5

Aboard the Underground Railroad

Towns and farms all across Ohio served as Underground Railroad stations. They were from 10 to 20 miles apart. Conductors ranged in age from teenage boys to older men and women. They guided fugitives from station to station. Some runaways walked. Others rode in wagons driven by white conductors. Sometimes they lay hidden in the bottom of a wagon, underneath sacks of farm produce.

Conductors worked separately. Sometimes members of the same family did not tell each other what they were doing. It was safer that way. No one could then tell on anyone else.

Runaways stayed hidden during the day. The greatest danger came from paid slave catchers and others who might be tempted to point them out and claim the reward.

In many free states, conductors and stationmasters used special signals. These indicated whether the station was safe or whether slave catchers were nearby. At night, a candle or lantern in a certain window meant "welcome." Another signal of welcome was a cloth tied to a gatepost.

Stationmasters did not always know when a group was coming. There would be a knock at the door. "Who's there?" The correct answer was, "A friend with friends." The door would open to welcome the runaways. The conductor would then disappear into the night.

Before the group left Ripley, abolitionist women made full skirts and sunbonnets for Rachel and Callie. These were clothes that free women would wear. The bonnets also helped to hide their faces. Seth and William wore the suits the Rankin boys had given them. If slave catchers saw them, they would look like a family of free people.

Runaways often wore clothing that helped to conceal their faces.

Callie's Story

I'll never forget that pretty dress! Specially after those raggedy ones I'd worn in the fields. One of the Ripley ladies showed me my fine self in a mirror. "If they only could see me at Hickory Creek," I thought. I didn't just look like a different person, I felt free!! I told Rachel to hold her head high and wear her bonnet proudly, but it was hard for her. She was so beaten down by life.

Martha's Story

Not like you, Callie. Nothing could beat you down. But, honey, them clothes you had at Hickory Creek was one of the saddest sights I ever seen. When you'd been in the house with Miss Laura, you got all the nice dresses that she'd wore out. When they sent you out to the fields, that all changed. Rough homespun clothes and no shoes. Your feet and skin turned hard as tree bark. Gone was my soft, little girl.

From Ripley, they traveled north across the state in a zigzag pattern. That made it harder for slave catchers or owners to follow them. They traveled to stations in Bethel, Williamsburg, and Xenia. One farmhouse near Greenfield, Ohio, was the center of a small African-American community. It had a room to hide runaways. Many stations had rooms hidden behind sliding panels. Runaways also hid in attics, haylofts, and cellars. Some stations had tunnels from the main house to barns or sheds, providing a quick escape route.

William's Story

So many people helped us, in spite of the danger. And they had to think quickly! At the Wests' farmhouse, we were eating supper when there was a knock at the door. It was two slave catchers. As we scurried up the back stairs, I heard Mr. West calmly offer them supper. Then he said he had seen a raggedy family go down the road two hours before. Of course, there was no one, but the slave catchers left quickly to chase them.

I finally felt free to let on I could read. I asked Mr. West if he had Mr. Frederick Douglass's fine abolitionist newspaper. Douglass was, and still is, one of my heroes. He escaped slavery and got to be famous. Found out Callie could read some too!

We moved on. I heard the conductor say that he had sent word to Isaac Bingham telling him to expect five "packages," four large and one small. That was the code for our group.

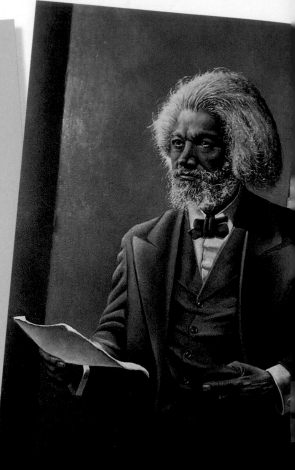

Frederick Douglass

Callie's Story

And, oh my, then it was September 21, a whole month since I'd run off. How my life had changed! Since slave hunters might be looking for two men, a woman, a girl, and a boy, I put on overalls and a straw hat and hoped I looked like a farm boy. Seth looked more different each day because he was growing a beard.

Rachel's boy made a lovely girl, though he squirmed at wearing a dress! He and our conductor could both pass as white. Rachel and William traveled as their servants. Now we didn't look like the folks the slave catchers were hunting.

$1200

TO

1250 DOLLARS

FOR NEGROES

NEGROES

WM. F. TALBOT

Runaways could hide in rooms behind secret doors. This door was hidden when the bed was moved in front of it.

Callie's Story

We hid in the Binghams' attic for eight days. Mrs. Bingham had baked plenty of bread and meat pies for us. She told folks they had measles in the house, so no one would come near. Still, I hated being shut up inside.

I learned more of Rachel's story. Her mother was a house servant, but Rachel worked in the fields 15 hours a day. She had no shoes and one change of clothing a year. Her husband was sold away. She never heard where he went.

From Westerville, near Columbus, the runaways traveled by canal boat on the Ohio and Erie Canal. Then they boarded a train. It took them almost to the shores of Lake Erie. Two Ohio port cities, Sandusky and Cleveland, were crossroads for the Underground Railroad. In the Underground Railroad code, Sandusky was "Sunrise." Cleveland was "Hope." Canada was only a few miles across Lake Erie. Canada meant real safety and freedom.

William's Story

I learned more about Seth too. He was a good person. I remember him saying, "I think we should be free because we ain't hogs or horses, we're humans." He came from a Tennessee plantation. Seth said he worked like a dog, 'cept the master's dog ate better than he did. When his master died, Seth was to be sent to his master's son-in-law in the South. He knew it was time to run.

I was happy to be back in a town. I liked the busy streets, the buildings, and the sounds I knew. It seemed that no one was following us. We stayed in a boarding house. There we got meals and beds. We lived like free people for the first time. I didn't know it, but we weren't through moving yet.

CHAPTER 6

Crossing to Canada

Many fugitives from the South lived in Sandusky, Ohio. Callie found work there as a cook. William worked for a printer in a newspaper office. A black Baptist minister and his family took in Rachel and her son. Rachel found she had a gift for healing and worked with the sick. Seth worked first for a farmer and then on the docks. Seth said he loved the smell of the lake. It was so different from the smell of the plantation.

Callie's Story

That was when I sent word to you again, Gramma, April of 1859. I had a place as a cook in a nice house. I used your recipes. It made me feel closer to you, but it made me miss you too. I wanted to tell you how it felt to earn wages and buy a new dress. I wanted you to know that things people said about the North weren't true. There were good, kind white folks as well as colored ones. I talked to you often in my head and heart.

Martha's Story

And you were in my heart too, girl. It was June when the preacher brought me word again. I was so happy to hear from you and think about you being free, my heart just 'bout burst. I felt proud that I had such a wonderful secret. I wanted to shout what I knew. I did let on to Miss Laura—kinda sideways like—that I'd heard good news about you, nothing that could get anyone in trouble. Still, I worried that I shouldn't have talked. But Miss Laura kept quiet. By then, she was in love with a Quaker boy herself. Her parents hated him. Things weren't real good at Hickory Creek then. Whenever I waited on table, I heard Master Henry and his friends arguing and carrying on about politics and war and all that.

Even in Sandusky, the runaways felt in danger. Slave catchers were always a threat. Callie and William carefully read the newspaper ads and posters for runaways. They wondered when they would find their names or those of Rachel or Seth.

William's Story

It finally happened. I remember the day, April 9, 1859. The ad was in the Saturday newspaper. "Reward: $800 for William Ballard, age 19, ran away from Elizabethtown, Kentucky. Thin, medium height, light-skinned, well-spoken, may be working in a store."

So Callie and I decided to join those who had gone to Canada. We traveled across Lake Erie to Windsor, Canada. Lucky for us that Seth was a deckhand on an "abolition boat." Good old Seth made sure we got there safely. The boat's captain was strongly antislavery. Rachel and her son stayed in Sandusky. No one would know her there. She'd become a strong, bold woman.

The boat landed at Windsor. In the Underground Railroad code, that city was known as "Glory to God." William went to work for the local printer and newspaper publisher. Seth decided to stay at his job on the abolition boat. Callie traveled to Elgin, a black settlement in what is now Ontario. With the money she had earned in Sandusky, Callie bought a cabin and some land for a vegetable garden.

The Elgin settlers built a school. There, Callie taught both children and adults to read and write. She and William kept in touch through letters. In 1864, when Callie was 20, they married. Seth took Rachel and her son to the wedding.

With the end of the Civil War and passage of the Thirteenth Amendment in 1865, all slaves were free. Callie and William then decided to return to the United States. The Homestead Act offered free land in the West to people who would live and farm there. The young couple settled in Nebraska with their children. Then they sent for Callie's Gramma. Now they were all free. With a sigh, they could tell their story about their time on the Underground Railroad.

Callie's children were among the first African Americans to go to college. All treasured a letter from their parents that they had been given one holiday.

Escaped slaves who settled in Windsor, Canada

July 4, 1870

Dear Children,
You know our stories about how we ran away. It is safe to share them now. Keep the stories close to your hearts. Share them with your children. Let them know how important freedom is. And how many people helped us gain it. Today, we celebrate when our country became free. It took us longer to be free. Never give up the right to freedom. Work to keep it. We love you.

Your parents,
Callie and William

Glossary

abolition–the ending of slavery

abolitionist–someone who wants to abolish, or end, slavery

ancestor–a person from whom one is descended

auction–a public sale in which goods or property are sold to the person who offers the most money

fugitive–a person who has run away

heritage–the traditions and skills passed down from one's ancestors

invest–to use money to buy something that is expected to make more money, or a profit

merchant–a person who buys and sells for profit

oral history–a history that is passed down from one generation to another

overseer–a person who directs the work of others

plantation–a large farm on which cotton, tobacco, sugar cane, or other crops are raised by people who live there

spiritual–a type of religious song that started among slaves

tradition–a belief, story, or custom handed down from parents to children

THIS BOOK BELONGS TO

_____

★ ★ ★ ★ ★ ★ ★ ★ ★ ★ ★ ★ ★